Followers to Friends

Build Authentic Connections and Lasting Success Online

Meek Dual

Copyright © 2024 Meek Dual

All rights reserved.

ISBN: 9798343971842

DEDICATION

To and for Pookie.

CONTENTS

PREFACE: *How to Get the Most from This Book* 1

    Why I Wrote This Book... 1

    How to Get the Most from This Book 2

    Reflect and Personalize 2

    Take Action... 2

    Track Your Progress.. 3

    Use the FREE Companion Workbook 3

    Evolve and Adapt.. 3

    What You'll Learn 3

    Your 90-Day Journey Begins Here 4

INTRODUCTION... 5

CHAPTER 1: *Understanding The Power of Trust Online* 9

    The Slow Burn of Building Trust 9

    Examples of Women Who Have Built Trust Over Time 10

    How to Build Trust with Your Own Audience............... 11

    Practical Self-Audit: What's Helping or Hurting Your Online Presence?.. 12

    Key Takeaway: Trust is the Key to Success 13

CHAPTER 2: *Crafting an Authentic Digital Persona* 15

    Why Authenticity Matters 15

    From Perfectly Curated to Real: How Authenticity Transformed Engagement 16

    Avoiding Over-Curation 17

    Showing Vulnerability 17

    Practical Tips for Defining and Sharing Your Core Values 18

    Key Takeaway: Authenticity is the Ultimate Magnet ... 20

CHAPTER 3: *Defining Your Audience and Niche* 21

    Why Knowing Your Audience is Key 21

    Understanding Who You're Trying to Reach 22

    Segmenting Your Audience: Emotional vs. Intellectual Engagement 23

    Real-World Examples: From Broad to Niche 24

    Practical Steps to Defining Your Niche 25

    Key Takeaway: Know Your Audience to Speak Their Language 27

CHAPTER 4: *The Art of Storytelling* 28

Why Stories Matter: Emotional Connection Equals Trust 28

The Power of Storytelling in Human Psychology 29

Real-World Examples: Storytelling that Built Loyal Audiences 30

How to Craft Stories that Reflect Your Journey and Your Audience's Needs 31

Key Takeaway: Stories Build Trust and Connection 34

CHAPTER 5: *Enhancing Perceived Value with Visual and Emotional Design* 35

Why Consistency is Key 35

The Power of Regular Communication: Stories of Success 36

Maintaining Consistency Without Burning Out 37

Practical Tips for Creating a Content Calendar 39

Key Takeaway: Consistency Fosters Trust and Engagement 41

CHAPTER 6: *Building Communities, Not Just Followers* ... 42

The Power of a Loyal Community 42

Building Private Communities Where Trust Thrives 43

Real-World Examples: From Influencers to Community Leaders 44

Practical Tips for Fostering Interaction in Online Communities 45

Key Takeaway: Communities Are Stronger Than Followers 48

CHAPTER 7: *Handling Criticism and Negative Feedback Gracefully*.......................... 49

The Power of Graceful Responses................ 49

Strategies for Responding to Criticism Constructively . 50

Turning Criticism Into Connection Opportunities 52

Creating a Feedback Strategy......................... 53

Key Takeaway: Grace Under Pressure Builds Trust....... 55

CHAPTER 8: *Building Trust Through Partnerships*............ 56

The Power of Partnerships 56

Choosing the Right Partners.......................... 57

Real-World Examples: Women Who Built Their Reputations Through Collaboration 59

How to Approach Potential Collaborators 60

Practical Tips for Building Mutually Beneficial Relationships 62

Key Takeaway: Collaborations Build Trust and Expand Influence.. 63

CHAPTER 9: *Measuring Your Impact and Growing with Integrity* 64

The Balance Between Data and Meaningful Engagement 64

How to Measure Engagement Beyond Likes and Shares 65

Stories of Growth by Focusing on Meaning Over Metrics 67

Growing with Integrity: Ethical Strategies for Sustainable Growth 68

Key Takeaway: Integrity Leads to Lasting Growth 71

CHAPTER 10: *Maintaining Momentum and Building Trust for the Long Term* 73

Trust as a Long-Term Relationship................................ 73

Staying Relevant Without Burnout 74

Stories of Long-Term Influencers Who Kept Their Communities Engaged... 74

Practical Tips for Developing a Long-Term Strategy 75

Key Takeaway: Trust is Built Through Consistency and Authenticity 78

CONCLUSION: *Building a Legacy of Trust* 79

The Foundations of Winning Hearts and Minds Online 80

A Call to Action: Your 90-Day Plan to Build Trust 82

BOOKS IN THIS SERIES: *The Course Creator's Toolkit* 84

Book 1: The Authority Advantage: Build Your Influence, Impact, and Income by Sharing What You Know 85

Book 2: Course Creator's Gold: Build Interactive Courses that Stick and SELL 86

Book 3: Followers to Friends: Build Authentic Connections and Lasting Success Online 88

ABOUT THE AUTHOR 90

ACKNOWLEDGMENTS

This book would not exist without the incredible support and patience of my clients, who have been with me through every twist and turn of this journey. To each of you who entrusted me with your visions, thank you for allowing me the space to experiment, grow, and fine-tune the very system I'm sharing in these pages.

You were my sounding boards, my inspiration, and sometimes (let's be honest) my guinea pigs. When things weren't quite perfect, you stayed the course. When I was figuring out what worked and what didn't, you stuck by me. Your trust gave me the courage to keep pushing forward, refining my process until it became something that I knew could help others.

I am deeply grateful for your belief in me, even when I didn't have all the answers (yet!). It's because of you that I was able to develop a system that's not just about growing numbers, but about growing relationships—authentic, meaningful connections that lead to lasting success. You are the reason I do this work, and your patience and faith mean the world to me.

This book is as much yours as it is mine, and I can't wait to see where we go from here. Thank you for allowing me to walk this journey with you—and for being the living proof that real, lasting success is built on trust, authenticity, and connection.

With gratitude,
Meek Dual

.

PREFACE:
How to Get the Most from This Book

Welcome to *Followers to Friends: Building Authentic Connections and Lasting Success Online.* If you're here, it's because you understand that the key to lasting success online isn't just about growing a follower count—it's about building real, authentic connections. Whether you're an entrepreneur, content creator, or a professional looking to expand your influence, this book is designed to help you cultivate trust and transform your audience from casual followers into loyal friends and supporters.

Why I Wrote This Book

After years of working with entrepreneurs, creators, and brands, I've seen one common challenge: people are great at attracting attention online, but they struggle with **building trust**. Many are focused on the numbers—follower count, likes, and shares—but those metrics alone don't guarantee success. True impact comes from fostering genuine relationships, creating valuable content, and showing up consistently in an authentic way.

That's why I wrote *Followers to Friends*. I want to help you move beyond vanity metrics and focus on what really matters: trust, loyalty, and community. When you build these foundations, your success becomes sustainable, and your influence becomes lasting.

How to Get the Most from This Book

To help you succeed in creating a loyal, engaged audience, this book is structured to give you actionable steps and practical strategies. Each chapter builds upon the last, guiding you through the process of establishing trust, creating meaningful connections, and growing a supportive community.

Here's how to get the most out of the journey:

Reflect and Personalize

As you read each chapter, take time to reflect on how the concepts apply to your unique situation. Whether it's identifying your audience's needs, sharing your personal story, or responding to feedback, think about how you can personalize each strategy for your brand. Every audience is different, and your approach should reflect your specific values and goals.

Take Action

This book is packed with actionable advice and practical exercises to help you implement the strategies. I encourage you to pause after each chapter and complete the exercises. Transformation happens when you take action, and these exercises are designed to move you forward in building trust and engagement with your audience.

Track Your Progress

Creating an authentic, loyal community takes time, and it's important to track your progress along the way. As you begin to apply the strategies from this book, take note of how your audience responds. Celebrate small wins—whether it's increased engagement, more meaningful conversations, or new relationships formed. Tracking your progress will allow you to see what's working and help you refine your approach over time.

Use the FREE Companion Workbook

To make your journey even easier, I've created a **FREE companion workbook** that includes additional exercises, templates, and planning tools to help you implement the strategies from this book. You can download it at meekdual.com/followerstofriends. The workbook is designed to help you stay organized, track your progress, and stay on course throughout your 90-day journey.

Evolve and Adapt

The online world is constantly changing, and so are your audience's needs. As you move forward, stay flexible and be willing to evolve. Trust is dynamic—it grows through consistent, meaningful interactions over time. Be open to learning, adapting, and improving as you continue to build your online presence.

What You'll Learn

In this book, you'll discover how to:

- **Build Trust**: Learn why trust is the foundation of any successful online relationship and how to establish it.

- **Share Your Story**: Craft your authentic digital persona to connect with your audience on a deeper level.

- **Create Engagement**: Develop strategies to foster consistent, meaningful engagement that goes beyond likes and shares.

- **Grow a Community**: Move beyond followers and build a loyal community that supports and champions your success.

- **Respond with Grace**: Learn how to handle criticism and feedback in a way that strengthens your credibility.

- **Leverage Partnerships**: Collaborate with trusted peers to expand your influence and grow your network.

Your 90-Day Journey Begins Here

Now that you have the roadmap, it's time to take action. Over the next 90 days, you have the opportunity to transform your online presence into a thriving, trusted community. Remember, this journey isn't about quick wins or overnight success—it's about building something real, sustainable, and meaningful. With the steps in this book and the **FREE companion workbook** to guide you, you'll have everything you need to succeed.

Let's dive in and start turning your followers into friends.

— Meek Dual

INTRODUCTION

Three years ago, Melody was just like you—trying to make sense of how to stand out online. She had a small Instagram following, posted regularly, and even tried engaging with her audience, but nothing seemed to move the needle. The more she tried to grow her presence, the more she felt like she was shouting into the void. Yet, in that same crowded space, she saw other women—women no more talented or hardworking than she was—building strong communities, gaining influence, and, most importantly, generating real income from their online presence. What was she doing wrong?

Melody's breakthrough came when she stopped focusing on numbers and started focusing on trust. She began sharing her story authentically, connecting with her audience on a deeper level, and providing value that spoke directly to their needs. Within months, Melody turned her modest following into a thriving community of loyal supporters—followers who not only engaged with her content but also became paying customers. Her online presence wasn't just about likes or comments anymore—it was about building genuine relationships that created real business opportunities.

If you're reading this, chances are you've felt that same frustration. You're putting in the work—posting consistently, following the trends, doing everything the "experts" say you should be doing—but your audience feels distant. Maybe you've grown your follower count, but when it comes to engagement, turning them into loyal customers, or creating sustainable income, you're not seeing the results you want.

The digital world is more crowded than ever. With millions of people vying for attention, how do you rise above the noise? How do you get people to care about what you're offering? How do you transform followers into real connections—ones that translate into trust, loyalty, and ultimately, wealth?

Imagine waking up to an inbox filled with messages from people who are genuinely interested in your products, services, or content. Picture creating posts that not only get likes but spark conversations and build a real connection with your audience. Better yet, imagine converting that engagement into real income streams—whether that's through selling products, offering services, or growing a personal brand that opens up countless opportunities.

This is not only possible—it's achievable within **90 days**. With the strategies I'm going to share in this book, you'll have the tools and confidence to build an online presence that doesn't just attract followers but turns them into loyal customers, true supporters, and lifelong advocates of your brand.

In the following chapters, you'll learn how to:

- **Build Trust**: Understand the foundations of trust online and why authenticity is your greatest asset.

- **Foster Engagement**: Discover the strategies to increase meaningful engagement with your audience and build a loyal community.

- **Grow Influence**: Learn how to turn your followers into advocates who not only engage with your content but support your business.

- **Monetize Your Audience**: Get the step-by-step guide on converting followers into paying customers and generating real income.

This isn't about gimmicks or shortcuts—it's about creating a sustainable, authentic presence that will help you grow both your audience and your wealth.

I know this process works because I've lived it. A few years ago, I was in your shoes—trying to figure out how to make a meaningful impact online. I started small, just like Melody, and like many of you, I struggled to gain traction. But once I shifted my focus from trying to "hack the algorithm" to building trust, everything changed. My audience grew, my engagement soared, and more importantly, my online presence became a real source of income.

Since then, I've helped countless women—entrepreneurs, influencers, and everyday people—transform their online presence into a thriving community of engaged, loyal followers. This book distills those lessons and provides a clear roadmap for you to follow.

Are you ready to take control of your online presence and turn followers into loyal supporters who will help drive your success? The journey may seem daunting, but I promise it's simpler than you think—especially when you focus on building genuine relationships.

In just **90 days**, you can change the way you approach social media, grow your influence, and most importantly, start generating wealth. So, let's get started. The road to building trust, engagement, and real business success online begins now.

Turn the page and let's win hearts and minds together.

CHAPTER 1:
Understanding The Power of Trust Online

If you've ever wondered why some online influencers seem to attract loyal followers so effortlessly while others struggle, the answer often boils down to one key factor: **trust**. Trust is the cornerstone of all successful online interactions. Without it, even the most well-crafted content will fail to resonate, and the biggest follower count will mean little if your audience doesn't truly believe in what you're offering.

The Slow Burn of Building Trust

Online trust isn't built overnight. It takes time, consistency, and, above all, authenticity. People can tell when something feels forced, and that's why shortcuts—like trying to grow through gimmicks, exaggerated claims, or paid followers—don't lead to sustainable success. Instead, real trust develops through repeated positive interactions, shared values, and honesty.

When we talk about trust, we often mean two distinct types: **emotional trust** and **informational trust**.

- **Emotional Trust**: This is the type of trust that forms when your audience feels a connection to you personally. They see your vulnerability, relate to your experiences, and feel that you understand their struggles. Emotional trust is built when you share your authentic self with your audience—whether that's talking about your challenges, celebrating your wins, or even admitting when things don't go as planned. It's about creating a relationship where your followers feel like they know you.

- **Informational Trust**: This form of trust is all about credibility. Does your audience believe the information you provide? Are you seen as a reliable source in your niche? Informational trust is built when you consistently share valuable, accurate, and actionable content. It's not about knowing everything but about providing honest insights that help your audience move forward.

Examples of Women Who Have Built Trust Over Time

Let's look at a couple of real-world examples of women who have successfully built both emotional and informational trust with their audiences.

Take **Jenna Kutcher**, for instance. Jenna started out as a wedding photographer but has since built a massive following by being unapologetically authentic. She shares everything from her personal struggles with body image to behind-the-scenes looks at running her business. Jenna's vulnerability builds emotional trust—her followers feel like they know the real Jenna, which is why they're loyal to her. At the same time, she offers tons of valuable business advice, free resources, and insights on entrepreneurship, building her informational trust.

Then there's **Marie Forleo**, a business coach and author who built her brand on giving rock-solid advice to aspiring entrepreneurs. Marie's followers trust her because she's consistent in delivering actionable steps and clear, effective strategies for success. Marie doesn't just show her expertise; she shows her humanity too, frequently sharing personal stories and encouraging her audience to embrace progress over perfection.

Both of these women took time to nurture relationships with their audiences. They didn't rush the process but focused on consistently showing up, providing value, and being real.

How to Build Trust with Your Own Audience

You don't have to be a massive influencer to start building trust online. In fact, you can begin right where you are by focusing on authenticity and consistency. Here are some practical tips for laying the foundation of trust with your audience:

1. **Be Consistent**: One of the quickest ways to break trust is inconsistency. When you disappear for weeks or constantly change your message, your audience feels uncertain. Create a content schedule that works for you, and stick to it. Whether it's posting once a week or sharing daily stories, show up when your audience expects you to.

2. **Show Your Vulnerable Side**: Don't be afraid to share your struggles or what you're working on behind the scenes. When you let people in on your

journey, they connect with you emotionally. Whether it's a failed project, a lesson learned, or a personal story, your authenticity will build emotional trust.

3. **Deliver Value**: It's not enough to just talk about yourself. You need to provide content that helps your audience solve a problem or see something in a new way. Share tips, offer insights, and give them information they can act on. Over time, your audience will come to rely on you as a trusted source of information.

4. **Be Honest**: If you don't know the answer to something, say so. If you make a mistake, own it. Transparency fosters trust. Your audience will appreciate your honesty and will respect you more for it.

Practical Self-Audit: What's Helping or Hurting Your Online Presence?

Before you can move forward with building trust, it's helpful to take a step back and evaluate where you are right now. Conducting a self-audit will help you identify what's currently working for you and what might be driving a wedge between you and your audience. Here's how to get started:

1. **Evaluate Your Content**: Take a look at your last ten posts. Do they reflect who you are and what you stand for? Are you offering value, or are you just going through the motions? If you feel like your content lacks depth, consider how you can bring more of your authentic self into your posts.

2. **Assess Your Engagement**: Are you responding to comments, messages, and questions from your audience? Engagement isn't just about posting; it's about being part of a conversation. If your followers feel like you're ignoring them, they'll be less likely to trust you. Make a point of replying to comments and fostering a dialogue with your community.

3. **Analyze Your Authenticity**: Are you being real with your audience, or are you presenting a filtered, "perfect" version of yourself? Authenticity doesn't mean oversharing, but it does mean being truthful about your experiences. If you've been overly curated in your posts, try loosening up and sharing more of your real life.

4. **Check Your Consistency**: Are you regularly showing up online, or do you disappear for long stretches? Consistency is key in maintaining trust. If you've been inconsistent, create a plan to post regularly in a way that feels sustainable for you.

By conducting a self-audit, you'll have a clearer idea of what's working and where you need to make adjustments to build stronger, more trusting relationships with your audience.

Key Takeaway: Trust is the Key to Success

Trust is the foundation of any meaningful online presence. It's the invisible thread that connects you to your audience, and it's what will set you apart in a crowded digital space. But remember, trust isn't built in a day—it's earned through your consistent actions and your willingness to show up authentically.

As you move forward, keep these lessons in mind and take small steps every day to nurture trust with your audience. The more you invest in building real relationships, the more your online presence will flourish, and your business will grow.

Now that you understand the power of trust, let's dive into how you can start crafting an authentic digital persona that will resonate deeply with your audience.

CHAPTER 2:
Crafting an Authentic Digital Persona

In a world where everyone is striving to be noticed, there's one thing that truly sets people apart online: **authenticity**. Authenticity is magnetic—it's what draws people in, makes them stay, and turns casual followers into loyal supporters. While it's easy to get caught up in curating the perfect image, the reality is that people crave real connections. Your audience is looking for someone they can relate to, someone who reflects their values and experiences.

Why Authenticity Matters

Your online persona is more than just the image you project—it's the core of how people perceive you and connect with you. But building an authentic digital presence is not about showing perfection. It's about showing up as yourself, in alignment with your values, and creating an online persona that feels both true to you and resonant with your audience.

When you try too hard to curate every post and present an idealized version of yourself, you risk losing that sense of realness that makes people trust you. Authenticity, on the other hand, fosters trust because it lets your audience see the human behind the brand. It tells them: *I'm not perfect, but I'm real. I'm like you.*

Your authenticity online needs to start with **alignment**—alignment between your personal values and what you share with the world. When you try to be something you're not, or when your online persona doesn't reflect your true self, your audience senses the disconnect. They'll notice the lack of depth in your posts, and it will be harder to build trust.

From Perfectly Curated to Real: How Authenticity Transformed Engagement

Let's take a look at two women who saw incredible shifts in their audience engagement when they traded perfection for authenticity.

Example 1: Rachel Hollis

Rachel Hollis, a successful entrepreneur and motivational speaker, was known for her polished content and perfectly curated images early on. But it wasn't until she posted a photo of herself in a bikini, showing off her stretch marks, that her following truly skyrocketed. Her message was clear: This is real life, and this is me. That vulnerable moment of raw authenticity spoke to millions of women who saw themselves in her story. It was proof that people connect more deeply when you embrace the imperfect parts of yourself, too.

Example 2: Glennon Doyle

Similarly, author and activist Glennon Doyle built her following by leaning into her real-life struggles, sharing stories of addiction, recovery, and divorce. Her audience didn't grow because she had a perfectly styled Instagram feed—it grew because her raw honesty gave her followers permission to be honest about their own struggles. Doyle's success proves that vulnerability is a powerful way to build a deep connection with your audience, and when people feel like they know the real you, they are far more likely to support you.

Avoiding Over-Curation

It's tempting to want to present your life, your brand, or your business in the best possible light. But **over-curation**—the practice of making everything look "perfect"—can actually drive a wedge between you and your audience. When every photo is perfectly styled, every caption overly polished, and every story carefully controlled, it's hard for your followers to see the real you.

Over-curation often creates a sense of distance between you and your audience. They may admire your content but struggle to feel a personal connection. They might even feel alienated, thinking, *I could never live up to that standard*. When you show your audience that your life, just like theirs, includes imperfections, you invite them to relate to you, which deepens their trust and engagement.

Showing Vulnerability

A key part of authenticity is vulnerability. Sharing not just your successes but also your struggles creates a deeper, more relatable connection with your audience. It's the moments when you show who you are behind the scenes—the challenges you've faced, the lessons you've learned—that resonate the most.

But showing vulnerability doesn't mean oversharing. It's about choosing moments that are relevant to your audience's journey. For example, if you're an entrepreneur, sharing a story about a time when you struggled to get your business off the ground can inspire others on similar paths. It's these moments that foster trust because they reveal that you, too, are human.

Practical Tips for Defining and Sharing Your Core Values

1. **Identify Your Core Values**:
   Before you can present an authentic digital persona, you need to be clear on what you stand for. What are the core values that guide your personal and professional life? Is it honesty, creativity, resilience, or community? Your values are the foundation of your brand, and everything you share online should align with them.

   - *Exercise*: Write down the five values that are most important to you. Then, think about how these values show up in your life and your work. Are they reflected in your content? If not, brainstorm ways you can bring them into your online presence.

2. **Share Stories That Reflect Those Values**:
   Once you're clear on your values, the next step is to communicate them through storytelling. Sharing personal anecdotes or lessons learned in line with

your values helps your audience understand who you are at your core.

- o *Example*: If one of your core values is resilience, you might share a story about a time when you faced a major challenge but kept going. This kind of storytelling helps your audience see that you live out your values and that you're someone they can relate to and trust.

3. **Be Intentional with Your Content**:
Everything you post online—whether it's a photo, a caption, or a video—should reflect the real you. That doesn't mean every post has to be serious or deeply personal, but it does mean that your content should be aligned with who you are.

- o *Tip*: As you create content, ask yourself: *Does this reflect my true self? Does it align with my core values? Will my audience connect with it on a personal level?* This practice will help ensure that your online presence remains authentic and true to you.

4. **Avoid Comparisons**:
One of the biggest pitfalls to authenticity is falling into the comparison trap. When you start comparing yourself to others online, it's easy to feel like you're not enough and to start imitating what's popular instead of what's true to you. Resist the urge to copy trends that don't align with your values or personality.

- *Reminder:* Your audience follows you because they're drawn to your unique voice and perspective. Focus on what makes you, *you*, rather than what's working for someone else.

Key Takeaway: Authenticity is the Ultimate Magnet

Your authentic digital persona is what will set you apart from everyone else online. By aligning your personal values with your content, avoiding the trap of over-curation, and showing vulnerability, you'll build an online presence that resonates deeply with your audience. Authenticity is magnetic—it draws people in and keeps them engaged because they can see the real you behind the posts.

In the next chapter, we'll explore how to take this authentic digital persona and connect it to your audience by defining your niche and understanding exactly who you're speaking to online.

CHAPTER 3:
Defining Your Audience and Niche

When it comes to building a meaningful online presence, one of the most critical steps is knowing **exactly** who you're speaking to. Without a clear understanding of your audience, your content risks being too broad, too generic, and too easily lost in the digital noise. But when you define your audience and carve out a specific niche, you can tailor your message, gain their trust, and foster deeper connections.

Why Knowing Your Audience is Key

The key to winning over any audience is speaking their language. To do that, you need to know who they are, what they care about, and what drives them. When you understand your audience deeply, you're able to address their pain points, answer their questions, and offer solutions that matter to them. This connection is what builds trust and loyalty.

A well-defined audience will also guide your content strategy, helping you to create messages that resonate rather than just casting a wide net and hoping something sticks.

When your audience feels like you're speaking directly to them, they're much more likely to engage, follow, and support you.

Understanding Who You're Trying to Reach

The first step in defining your audience is understanding their core characteristics. Who are they? What stage of life are they in? What are their challenges? What do they need help with?

Creating an **audience avatar**—a detailed profile of your ideal follower or customer—will help clarify who you're trying to reach. This avatar should represent the kind of person who would most benefit from your content, products, or services. When building your avatar, consider the following:

- **Demographics**: Age, gender, location, education, occupation, and income level.

- **Psychographics**: Values, interests, hobbies, and lifestyle.

- **Challenges**: What are their biggest pain points or problems? What keeps them up at night?

- **Goals**: What do they hope to achieve, and how can you help them get there?

Let's imagine you're a wellness coach targeting women who are juggling careers and family life. Your audience avatar might be a 35-year-old working mother who feels overwhelmed by stress and struggles to find time for self-care. She's looking for simple, realistic ways to improve her health and wellness without adding to her already-full plate.

Segmenting Your Audience: Emotional vs. Intellectual Engagement

It's also important to understand how different segments of your audience engage with your content. Generally, your audience will fall into two broad categories: those who engage **emotionally** and those who engage **intellectually**.

- **Emotionally Engaged Audience**: These followers connect with your content on a personal or emotional level. They may relate to your struggles, feel inspired by your story, or resonate with your vulnerability. For them, your authenticity is what draws them in. They're looking for emotional connection, inspiration, and reassurance that they're not alone.

- **Intellectually Engaged Audience**: These followers are drawn to the value of your information. They're looking for expert advice, tips, strategies, and solutions. They care about the facts and want actionable insights that will help them achieve their goals. For them, you're a trusted authority, and they follow you because they know they'll learn something valuable.

Understanding this distinction allows you to tailor your content. For emotionally engaged audiences, share personal stories, behind-the-scenes insights, or reflections on your journey. For intellectually engaged audiences, focus on tips, how-tos, and solutions to their problems.

Real-World Examples: From Broad to Niche

Some of the most successful women in the online space have found their audience and built deep engagement by narrowing their focus and shifting from broad content to a defined niche. Here are two examples:

Example 1: Melissa, a Fitness Influencer Melissa started as a general fitness influencer, posting about everything from workout routines to nutrition tips. She gained followers but struggled to turn them into a loyal community. Realizing that her content was too broad, she decided to focus specifically on postpartum fitness for new mothers. By narrowing her niche, she was able to speak directly to her audience's specific needs—helping women regain strength and confidence after childbirth. Her engagement skyrocketed as she became a trusted source for her niche audience, and her followers started referring her content to others, leading to exponential growth.

Example 2: Kayla, a Business Coach Kayla initially offered business coaching to all types of entrepreneurs, from freelancers to CEOs. Her message lacked clarity, and she had difficulty creating consistent engagement. After analyzing her audience and defining her niche, she decided to focus exclusively on helping female solopreneurs grow online businesses. With this shift, Kayla started to create content that spoke directly to the challenges and goals of her new, more specific audience. As a result, her trust and credibility grew, and her business flourished.

These examples show that by honing in on a specific niche, you can better align your content with your audience's needs, leading to stronger connections and greater success.

Practical Steps to Defining Your Niche

1. **Research Your Audience's Pain Points**:
   Start by identifying the problems your audience faces. What challenges are they dealing with? What questions are they asking? You can find this information by conducting surveys, joining online communities where your audience hangs out, or simply by engaging with your current followers.

   o *Tip*: Check forums, social media comments, and other discussion platforms to find out what people in your niche are talking about. What are their frustrations, and how can you solve them?

2. **Assess Your Strengths and Passions**:
   Your niche should align with your own expertise and interests. What are you passionate about, and where do your skills lie? When you're creating content that excites you, it will resonate more with your audience.

   o *Exercise*: Write down your top skills and interests. Then, consider how you can combine them to serve a specific audience. For example, if you're a graphic designer passionate about eco-friendly living, your niche might be helping sustainable businesses with branding and design.

3. **Evaluate the Market:**

   Research your competition. Who else is serving this audience? Are there gaps in the content they're offering that you can fill? Finding a unique angle or underserved niche can set you apart in a crowded market.

   - *Tip*: Don't be afraid to get specific. Narrowing your focus can feel risky, but it often leads to stronger engagement because you're addressing a particular need.

4. **Create an Audience Avatar:**

   Once you've researched and defined your niche, create a detailed profile of your ideal audience member. This avatar will serve as a reference point as you develop content, ensuring you're always speaking to the right people.

   - *Example*: If you're a finance coach targeting millennials struggling with debt, your audience avatar might be a 29-year-old professional earning a decent salary but overwhelmed by student loans and credit card debt. They're looking for simple, step-by-step strategies to get out of debt and build wealth.

5. **Test and Refine:**

   Once you've defined your niche and started creating content for your target audience, pay attention to how your audience responds. Are they engaging with your content? Are you attracting the right followers?

Don't be afraid to tweak your approach based on what resonates most.

- o *Reminder*: Defining your niche isn't a one-time process. It evolves as you grow and learn more about your audience. Be flexible and willing to make adjustments along the way.

Key Takeaway: Know Your Audience to Speak Their Language

Understanding who you're trying to reach is the foundation of building trust and fostering engagement online. By defining your audience and narrowing your niche, you can speak directly to their needs, build stronger connections, and grow a loyal community. The more specific you are about who you serve and what you offer, the more powerful your message will become.

In the next chapter, we'll explore how to leverage the power of storytelling to connect with your audience on an emotional level and deepen the trust you've built.

CHAPTER 4:
The Art of Storytelling

If there's one thing that has the power to connect people across time, cultures, and backgrounds, it's storytelling. Stories have been used for centuries to pass down knowledge, share experiences, and connect emotionally with others. When it comes to building an online presence, storytelling is one of the most powerful tools you can use to build trust and foster deep relationships with your audience.

Why Stories Matter: Emotional Connection Equals Trust

At its core, storytelling is about connection. When you share a story, you invite your audience into your world. You're not just telling them what you do or what you offer—you're showing them who you are, what you stand for, and why they should care. This emotional connection is what makes people more likely to trust you and support your brand.

The psychology behind storytelling is simple but powerful. Stories tap into the emotional centers of the brain, making your audience feel rather than just think. This emotional engagement is critical for building relationships, as it creates a sense of shared experience and understanding. People are far more likely to remember and relate to a story than to a list of facts or a sales pitch. When your audience feels emotionally connected to your story, they're more likely to trust you and, ultimately, more likely to buy from you, follow you, and advocate for your brand.

The Power of Storytelling in Human Psychology

Our brains are hardwired for stories. Studies show that when we hear a story, we engage in **narrative transportation**—a phenomenon where the listener becomes so engrossed in the story that they feel as though they are part of it. This is what makes storytelling so effective in creating lasting impressions and emotional bonds.

When you tell a story, your audience isn't just listening; they're feeling the emotions, visualizing the details, and relating it to their own experiences. This leads to a deeper connection and a stronger sense of trust because your audience begins to see you not just as a content creator, but as someone who understands their struggles, hopes, and dreams.

In the context of building an online audience, this means that your stories can make you more relatable, authentic, and trustworthy. Whether you're sharing a personal struggle, a success, or a lesson learned, your story has the power to create an emotional bridge between you and your audience.

Real-World Examples: Storytelling that Built Loyal Audiences

Let's take a look at a couple of real-world examples of women who have used the power of storytelling to build loyal followers and thriving online communities.

Example 1: Brené Brown

Brené Brown is a renowned researcher and author, known for her work on vulnerability and courage. While she has a background in research, it's her ability to share personal stories that has endeared her to millions. By openly discussing her struggles with shame, perfectionism, and vulnerability, Brené has connected with her audience on a deeply personal level. Her TED Talks and books are filled with stories from her own life, which make her research feel relatable and real. It's her storytelling that has turned her into a household name, and her audience feels connected to her not just as a scholar but as a person who understands their challenges.

Example 2: Humans of New York (HONY)

Humans of New York (HONY) began as a simple photography project, but it quickly became a worldwide phenomenon because of the way it used storytelling. Instead of just sharing pictures, HONY shared the stories of everyday people in New York City. These stories—sometimes sad, sometimes hopeful, always real—touched millions of people. By telling the intimate, personal stories of strangers, HONY created a massive following of people who felt emotionally connected to the lives of others. It's a perfect example of how powerful stories can be when they resonate on a human level.

Both of these examples highlight the immense impact storytelling can have on building an engaged, loyal audience. When people connect emotionally to your story, they're far more likely to stay with you, trust you, and support your mission.

How to Craft Stories that Reflect Your Journey and Your Audience's Needs

Crafting a compelling story for your audience isn't about having the most dramatic life experiences or crafting the most perfectly written narrative. It's about **authenticity** and **relevance**—sharing stories that reflect your own journey while also speaking to your audience's needs, challenges, and aspirations.

Here's how to get started:

1. **Know Your Purpose**

    Every story should have a clear purpose. Ask yourself: *Why am I telling this story?* Are you trying to inspire? Educate? Build connection? Your story should serve both you and your audience, providing a lesson or insight that aligns with your values and their needs. Whether it's a personal anecdote or a professional experience, your story should reflect a larger theme that's important to your audience.

    o *Example*: If you're a business coach and you want to show your audience that failure is part of the journey to success, you might share a story about a time when one of your projects failed, what you learned from it, and how it helped you grow.

2. **Be Vulnerable**

   Vulnerability is the cornerstone of meaningful storytelling. Don't be afraid to share your struggles, failures, or moments of uncertainty. Your audience wants to know that you're human, just like them. It's often the imperfect, raw moments that resonate the most. Being open about your challenges shows your audience that you're real, and it invites them to connect with you on a deeper level.

   - *Tip*: Share a story about a time when you faced a setback or challenge and what you learned from it. Be honest about how it made you feel and how you overcame it. This will help your audience see you as relatable and trustworthy.

3. **Make It Relatable**

   While your story should reflect your personal journey, it should also speak to your audience's experiences. Think about what your audience is going through—what challenges they face, what questions they have, what fears they hold. When you frame your story in a way that mirrors their struggles, it becomes more than just your story—it becomes theirs too.

   - *Tip*: After telling your story, tie it back to your audience's journey. For example, if you're sharing a story about building your business, talk about how your audience can use your experience to overcome similar challenges in their own lives.

4. **Show, Don't Just Tell**

   One of the key rules of storytelling is to show, not just tell. Instead of saying, "I was overwhelmed," describe the situation in a way that lets your audience feel it. What were you doing? How did it look or sound? What did you feel physically and emotionally? Painting a vivid picture allows your audience to step into your shoes and experience the moment with you.

   - *Example*: Instead of simply saying, "I was stressed," you might say, "I sat at my desk, staring at the endless to-do list, my hands shaking as the clock ticked past midnight." This type of description brings your story to life.

5. **Keep It Concise and Focused**

   While stories can be powerful, they should also be focused. Don't get lost in too many details or off-topic tangents. Keep your story clear and concise, sticking to the central theme that you want your audience to take away. This helps your message stay impactful and memorable.

   - *Tip*: After writing your story, read through it and remove any unnecessary details or distractions. Make sure every part of the story serves your purpose and keeps your audience engaged.

○

Key Takeaway: Stories Build Trust and Connection

Storytelling is one of the most powerful ways to build trust and deepen your connection with your audience. By sharing personal, relatable, and emotionally resonant stories, you allow your audience to see the real you—and that's what keeps them coming back for more.

As you move forward in your journey, think about how you can use storytelling to not only share your experiences but to connect with your audience on a deeper, more personal level. The more authentic and vulnerable you are in your storytelling, the more trust you'll build.

In the next chapter, we'll dive into the power of engagement—how to not only tell your story but also listen and respond to your audience in ways that keep them coming back.

CHAPTER 5:
Enhancing Perceived Value with Visual and Emotional Design

Consistency is the lifeblood of building trust online. When you communicate regularly with your audience, they begin to rely on you—and that reliability fosters deeper connections and trust. In a world where audiences are bombarded with endless content, consistency is what keeps you top-of-mind. Your audience knows when and where to find you, and they begin to see you as a dependable source of value. **Consistency builds reliability, and reliability builds trust.**

Why Consistency is Key

The online space moves fast. If you disappear for too long or post sporadically, your audience may lose interest or forget about you altogether. Regular communication reassures your audience that you're invested in the relationship, and that you're here to stay. Consistent interaction also reinforces your brand and message, helping you build a more recognizable and trusted presence.

But beyond just posting regularly, **transparent communication** is equally important. Being open with your audience about your journey, your successes, and even your challenges helps build a genuine sense of community. When your audience knows they can expect honesty from you, they become more loyal and engaged. People appreciate authenticity, but they also appreciate knowing that you're someone they can count on.

The Power **of Regular Communication: Stories of Success**

Many women who have successfully built engaged, loyal followings did so by shifting from sporadic posting to consistent, transparent communication.

Example 1: Luvvie Ajayi Jones

Luvvie, a bestselling author and digital strategist, grew her audience by regularly showing up and offering her unique perspective on culture and social justice. Initially, she posted inconsistently and wasn't seeing much growth. But once she committed to a consistent content schedule, including weekly blog posts and regular social media updates, her audience grew significantly. Luvvie didn't just post for the sake of posting—she made sure each piece of content was meaningful, aligned with her values, and invited engagement. Today, her consistency and transparency have turned her into a trusted voice with a highly engaged following.

Example 2: Jenna Kutcher

Jenna Kutcher, a successful entrepreneur and podcast host, admits that she didn't always have a content strategy. Early in her journey, she posted inconsistently, and her engagement fluctuated as a result. But once she implemented a structured content calendar, things changed. She committed to showing up consistently on her podcast, blog, and Instagram, creating a blend of personal stories, valuable business advice, and audience-driven content. The results? Her audience grew exponentially, and so did their loyalty. Jenna's followers know they can count on her to deliver content that speaks to their needs, and her regular communication fosters a strong sense of community.

These stories illustrate the transformative power of regular and transparent communication. Consistency helps you establish a rhythm with your audience, while transparency fosters trust and connection.

Maintaining Consistency Without Burning Out

Of course, maintaining a consistent content schedule can feel overwhelming, especially if you're juggling other responsibilities. The key is finding a balance that works for you and ensures that you stay engaged without burning out. Here's how you can maintain consistent communication while staying true to yourself:

1. **Set a Realistic Content Schedule**
   Consistency doesn't mean you have to post every day. It's more important to choose a schedule that you can maintain long-term. Whether it's posting three times a week or publishing a weekly newsletter, the goal is to stick to a rhythm that keeps you connected to your audience.

   o *Tip*: Start with a realistic frequency, and then scale up if you feel comfortable. It's better to post once a week consistently than to post every day for two weeks and then disappear for a month.

2. **Leverage Multiple Platforms**
Your audience likely engages with content across different platforms, so it's important to diversify where and how you communicate. Whether it's Instagram, YouTube, a blog, or an email list, try to maintain a presence on the platforms where your audience is most active. But remember, you don't need to be everywhere all at once. Focus on mastering one or two platforms before expanding to others.

    o *Tip*: Repurpose content across platforms. A blog post can become an Instagram caption, a podcast can be turned into a YouTube video, and a series of tweets can be expanded into a newsletter. This approach saves time and keeps your messaging consistent across channels.

3. **Plan Ahead with a Content Calendar**
One of the best ways to stay consistent is to plan ahead. A content calendar helps you organize your ideas, map out your posts, and ensure that you're balancing personal stories, valuable insights, and audience engagement. With a content calendar, you won't be scrambling for ideas at the last minute—your content will be intentional and aligned with your overall strategy.

o   *Tip*: Use a simple tool like Google Calendar, Trello, or even a paper planner to schedule your content for the month. Decide in advance what topics you'll cover, what formats you'll use (video, blog, etc.), and which platforms you'll publish on.

4. **Balance Personal Stories and Valuable Content**
   It's important to strike a balance between sharing your personal journey and providing valuable content that addresses your audience's needs. Your audience wants to get to know you, but they also want content that benefits them. By mixing personal stories with practical advice, you create a connection while positioning yourself as a trusted source of value.

   o   *Example*: If you're a business coach, you might share a personal story about a challenge you faced while growing your business, and then offer actionable tips on how your audience can overcome a similar challenge. This combination of storytelling and value keeps your content engaging and relevant.

Practical Tips for Creating a Content Calendar

1. **Choose Your Key Themes**
   Start by identifying the key themes you want to focus on in your content. These should align with your audience's needs and your personal or business goals. For example, if you're a wellness coach, your

themes might include stress management, self-care routines, and nutrition tips.

- o *Tip*: Limit yourself to 3-5 core themes. This will help keep your content focused and ensure that everything you post aligns with your overall message.

2. **Map Out Your Content**

Once you've chosen your themes, map out your content for the upcoming month. Decide how often you'll post and what type of content you'll create (blog posts, videos, social media updates, etc.). Be sure to include a mix of personal stories, valuable insights, and engagement-driven content (such as Q&A sessions or polls).

- o *Tip*: Assign specific topics to each week. For example, Week 1 might focus on storytelling, Week 2 on a how-to guide, Week 3 on audience engagement, and Week 4 on sharing your personal journey. This variety keeps your content fresh and interesting.

3. **Automate and Schedule**

To make the process easier, use automation tools to schedule your posts in advance. Platforms like Buffer, Hootsuite, or Later allow you to schedule social media posts, while tools like Mailchimp or ConvertKit can help you automate your email newsletters.

- o *Tip*: Set aside a specific day each week or month to create and schedule your content in batches. This ensures you always have something ready to go, even during busy times.

4. **Engage with Your Audience**
   Consistent communication isn't just about posting—it's also about engaging with your audience. Respond to comments, answer questions, and encourage conversation. The more engaged your audience feels, the more likely they are to stay connected and trust you.

   - *Tip*: Dedicate a few minutes each day to respond to comments or messages. Even a quick reply can make your audience feel valued and seen.

Key Takeaway: Consistency Fosters Trust and Engagement

Consistency is the secret to building a loyal, engaged audience. By maintaining a regular content schedule and balancing personal stories with valuable insights, you create a reliable and authentic presence that your audience can trust. Remember, it's not about being perfect—it's about showing up, being transparent, and keeping the lines of communication open.

In the next chapter, we'll explore how to take the community you've built and transform it into a loyal, engaged group of followers who support you not just online, but in your business as well.

CHAPTER 6:
Building Communities, Not Just Followers

In the fast-paced world of social media, followers come and go, and platforms rise and fall. But a strong, loyal **community** outlasts trends, algorithms, and even platforms themselves. While having a large following can seem like the ultimate goal, what truly matters is building a community of people who are deeply engaged and connected with your mission. **Strong, trusting communities outlast trends and platforms** because they are built on shared values, trust, and meaningful interaction—not just fleeting attention.

The Power of a Loyal Community

The difference between followers and a community lies in engagement. **Followers** might like your posts or watch your videos, but a **community** actively participates, supports, and advocates for you. A large but disengaged following can be shallow—full of people who see your content but don't connect with it on a deeper level. In contrast, a small but engaged community can generate more meaningful interactions, lead to higher conversion rates, and provide long-term support for your brand or business.

The secret to building this kind of community is trust. When people feel like they're part of something bigger, that their voice matters, and that there's a genuine connection between them and the leader of the group, they're more likely to engage and stay loyal over time. **A loyal community is far more powerful than a large but disengaged following.**

Building Private Communities Where Trust Thrives

One of the best ways to cultivate deep connections with your audience is by creating **private communities** where engagement is more personal and direct. Platforms like Facebook groups, email lists, or membership sites allow you to move beyond the public nature of social media and build a space where your audience feels more connected and valued.

- **Facebook Groups**: A private Facebook group offers an intimate space where your audience can interact with you and with each other. Unlike public social media platforms, where posts can get lost in the algorithm, Facebook groups prioritize member posts, meaning conversations are more likely to be seen and responded to. These groups are also great for fostering interaction, as members feel they're part of an exclusive community with shared interests.

- **Email Lists**: While social media platforms can change their algorithms at any time (and you don't own your followers on these platforms), your email list is something you control. Building a strong email list allows you to communicate directly with your audience, offer personalized content, and deepen relationships over time. It's one of the most effective ways to cultivate trust and keep your community engaged, even if social media platforms shift.

- **Membership Sites or Private Forums**: For those looking to build a more exclusive or premium community, membership sites or private forums can offer a space where your most dedicated followers can interact, access premium content, and participate in discussions. These spaces often foster even deeper engagement, as members feel a greater sense of commitment to the group.

Real-World Examples: From Influencers to Community Leaders

Many successful women have shifted their focus from amassing followers to cultivating meaningful communities, and the results have been transformative.

Example 1: Marie Forleo

Marie Forleo, a business coach and the founder of B-School, is known not just for her large following but for the strong community she has built around her educational programs. Marie's focus isn't just on teaching—she's created a thriving community of like-minded entrepreneurs who support each other. Through her private Facebook groups, exclusive content, and direct interaction with her students, Marie has fostered a loyal community of people who continue to engage with her long after the initial sale. Her focus on community over simple follower count has allowed her business to flourish and her students to become advocates for her brand.

Example 2: Melyssa Griffin

Melyssa Griffin started out as a blogger and quickly grew her following by offering helpful resources on blogging and business. But it wasn't until she shifted her focus from building a following to creating an engaged community that her brand truly took off. Melyssa launched a private Facebook group where she regularly interacted with her audience, hosted challenges, and fostered a space where members could support each other. This shift from influencer to community leader helped her build deeper relationships with her audience and transform her brand into a thriving business, with a dedicated group of loyal supporters.

Both of these women recognized that having a large following wasn't enough—they needed to create a space where trust, engagement, and genuine relationships could thrive. By focusing on community-building, they were able to transform their online presence into something far more powerful and long-lasting.

Practical Tips for Fostering Interaction in Online Communities

1. **Create a Welcoming Space**
   Whether you're building a Facebook group, growing an email list, or launching a membership site, the first step is to create a welcoming, inclusive space where your audience feels comfortable engaging. Set the tone by being approachable and encouraging

participation. Introduce yourself, share your mission, and make it clear that everyone's voice matters.

- o *Tip*: In a Facebook group, you could start by welcoming new members with a personalized post and encouraging them to introduce themselves. In an email list, send a welcome email that sets expectations and invites subscribers to respond with their thoughts or questions.

2. **Encourage Interaction with Open-Ended Questions**

   One of the easiest ways to foster interaction in a community is by asking open-ended questions that invite members to share their thoughts, experiences, and ideas. Questions spark conversation and allow members to connect with each other on a deeper level.

   - o *Example*: If you're running a wellness community, you could ask, "What's one challenge you've faced this week in staying healthy, and how did you overcome it?" Questions like this encourage members to share personal stories, which builds a sense of community.

3. **Host Regular Live Interactions**

   Live interactions, whether it's through video sessions, Q&A events, or live chats, allow your community to engage with you in real time. These interactions build a stronger sense of connection and make your community feel more personal. Live sessions also give you the chance to answer questions, offer valuable insights, and foster engagement.

- o *Tip*: Host a monthly live Q&A session where you address your audience's most pressing questions. This not only provides value but also deepens the sense of connection between you and your community.

4. **Promote Peer-to-Peer Support**
A thriving community isn't just about you interacting with your audience—it's also about creating a space where your audience can connect with and support each other. Encourage peer-to-peer interaction by creating opportunities for members to share their own experiences, advice, and ideas.

- o *Tip*: In a Facebook group, create themed days where members can post their questions, wins, or challenges. For example, "Win Wednesday" could be a day when members share their recent accomplishments, and other members can celebrate with them.

5. **Reward and Recognize Engagement**
People love to feel valued and appreciated. Acknowledge your most active or helpful members by recognizing them publicly or offering small rewards for their contributions. This recognition not only encourages more engagement but also shows

your community that you care about their involvement.

- *Tip*: Give a "Member of the Month" shoutout in your community, highlighting someone who has been particularly active, helpful, or engaged. You could also offer small incentives like exclusive content or a free consultation.

Key Takeaway: Communities Are Stronger Than Followers

Building a loyal, engaged community is far more valuable than simply accumulating followers. A community is built on trust, shared values, and meaningful interaction—and it outlasts social media trends or algorithm changes. By fostering a sense of connection and creating a space where your audience feels valued, you can turn followers into a community that supports, engages, and advocates for you.

In the next chapter, we'll discuss how to handle criticism and negative feedback with grace, and how to turn even the toughest challenges into opportunities to deepen trust with your audience.

CHAPTER 7:
Handling Criticism and Negative Feedback Gracefully

No matter how thoughtfully you build your online presence, criticism and negative feedback are inevitable. As your audience grows, so too will the diversity of opinions about your content, your message, and even you personally. While it's never easy to receive harsh feedback, how you respond to it can either reinforce or erode the trust you've worked so hard to build. **Trust is tested in how you handle criticism**, and responding with grace and integrity can turn difficult moments into opportunities for connection.

The Power of Graceful Responses

Criticism, especially online, can feel personal and hurtful. It's easy to take negative feedback to heart, but responding defensively or with anger can damage your reputation and push your audience away. On the other hand, handling criticism with grace can build credibility, solidify trust, and even win over some of your harshest critics.

When you address negative feedback constructively, it shows that you're open to listening, willing to improve, and confident enough to handle disagreement. **Gracefully addressing negative feedback builds credibility and solidifies trust** because it demonstrates maturity, professionalism, and respect for differing perspectives.

Strategies for Responding to Criticism Constructively

There's an art to responding to criticism in a way that protects both your brand and your peace of mind. Here are some key strategies for navigating negative feedback:

1. **Pause Before You React**
   When you first receive negative feedback, your initial reaction might be to defend yourself or even fire back. However, responding emotionally in the heat of the moment rarely ends well. Instead, take a step back and give yourself time to process the criticism. This pause allows you to respond thoughtfully rather than react impulsively.

   - *Tip*: If you find yourself feeling triggered by a negative comment, take a deep breath, and wait at least 24 hours before responding. This gives you time to assess the situation objectively and decide on the best course of action.

2. **Acknowledge the Criticism**
   Whether or not you agree with the feedback, it's important to acknowledge it. Ignoring criticism can make you seem dismissive or unwilling to listen, which can hurt your credibility. By acknowledging

the feedback, you show that you respect your audience's opinions, even if they're not always positive.

- *Example*: A simple acknowledgment like, "Thank you for sharing your thoughts. I appreciate your feedback and will take it into consideration," can go a long way in showing that you value input, even when it's difficult to hear.

3. **Find the Constructive Elements**

   Not all criticism is constructive, but there are often valuable lessons buried beneath the harsh words. If the feedback is specific, use it as an opportunity to improve. Ask yourself, *Is there truth in this feedback? Is there something I can do better?* By seeing criticism as an opportunity for growth, you can turn a negative situation into a learning experience.

   - *Tip*: If a follower points out an error or makes a valid suggestion for improvement, publicly thank them for bringing it to your attention. This not only builds trust but shows your commitment to continual growth.

4. **Respond with Empathy**

   Responding to criticism with empathy can diffuse tension and help you build a deeper connection with your audience. Try to see the situation from the critic's perspective—are they frustrated? Do they feel misunderstood? A response that shows you've taken their feelings into account can turn a negative situation into a positive one.

- o *Example*: Instead of defending yourself, you might say, "I can see why you feel that way, and I appreciate you sharing your perspective. I'll keep that in mind as I continue to improve."

5. **Know When to Let It Go**
Not all criticism deserves a response. Some feedback may come from trolls or people simply looking to stir up negativity. In these cases, it's important to recognize when it's best to let go and move on. Engaging with people whose only goal is to provoke you can waste your time and energy while dragging you into unnecessary drama. Sometimes, the best response is no response at all.

- o *Tip*: If a comment is blatantly rude, personal, or inflammatory, consider deleting it or ignoring it altogether. Focus on engaging with constructive feedback that helps you grow.

Turning Criticism Into Connection Opportunities

Some of the most successful women online have turned harsh criticism into opportunities to connect with their audience on a deeper level. They didn't shy away from tough feedback—instead, they embraced it as a chance to show humility, honesty, and strength.

Example 1: Taylor Swift's Shift in Public Perception

Taylor Swift faced significant public criticism in the wake of several high-profile media controversies. Rather than retaliate defensively, she took time away to reflect and then returned to the public eye with a new, more self-aware approach. By addressing the criticism head-on, acknowledging her mistakes, and expressing her growth, she regained the trust of many fans and even won over some of her critics. Taylor's ability to handle criticism gracefully played a major role in reshaping her public image.

Example 2: Jameela Jamil's Transparent Approach
Jameela Jamil, actress and activist, is known for her outspoken views on body positivity and diet culture. When she was publicly criticized for past comments and positions, Jameela didn't shy away from the feedback. Instead, she engaged in meaningful conversations with her critics, admitting when she had been wrong and using her platform to show her evolution. This transparency turned what could have been a divisive situation into an opportunity for connection, and her audience respected her even more for her willingness to listen and grow.

Creating a Feedback Strategy

To handle criticism effectively, it's important to develop a strategy for how you'll respond to feedback. This ensures you're prepared when the inevitable negative comment or review comes your way.

1. **Set Guidelines for Your Responses**
   Decide in advance how you'll respond to different types of criticism. For constructive feedback, plan to acknowledge and engage. For destructive comments, decide whether you'll ignore, delete, or respond

briefly. Having a plan in place will help you stay calm and consistent in your approach.

- o *Tip*: Draft template responses for common criticisms or concerns. This way, you're prepared and can respond quickly while maintaining your professionalism.

2. **Create Personal Boundaries**
It's important to protect your mental and emotional health when dealing with criticism online. Set clear boundaries about what kinds of feedback you're willing to engage with and when you need to step away. Remember that it's okay to protect yourself from toxic negativity.

- o *Tip*: Schedule regular social media breaks or designate specific times to check comments and messages. This will prevent you from becoming overwhelmed by feedback and give you time to process before responding.

3. **Encourage Constructive Feedback**
Invite your audience to share their thoughts in a way that encourages productive conversation rather than hostility. By creating a culture of constructive feedback, you can foster a space where criticism is shared respectfully and with the intent to improve, rather than attack.

- o *Tip*: When asking for feedback, be specific. Instead of saying, "What did you think of this?" ask, "What's one thing I could improve in my next project?" This invites helpful input and sets the tone for respectful dialogue.

Key Takeaway: Grace Under Pressure Builds Trust

How you handle criticism is a reflection of your character and professionalism. When you respond with grace, empathy, and a willingness to learn, you show your audience that you value their input and are committed to growth. Criticism, though uncomfortable, is an opportunity to build credibility and deepen trust with your community.

In the next chapter, we'll explore the importance of collaboration and networking, and how building partnerships with like-minded people can strengthen your brand and expand your influence online.

CHAPTER 8:
Building Trust Through Partnerships

When it comes to growing your online presence and building trust, one of the most effective strategies is **collaboration**. Partnering with other trusted peers, influencers, or brands not only amplifies your reach but also enhances your credibility. **Collaborating with trusted peers builds your credibility** by associating you with others who already have established trust with their own audiences. When done authentically, partnerships can exponentially grow your audience's trust in you and expand your influence in ways that are mutually beneficial for all involved.

The Power of Partnerships

Partnerships are a powerful way to grow because they allow you to leverage someone else's audience while bringing value to your own. When you collaborate with someone who has built their own reputation and trust, their audience is more likely to view you favorably, simply because of the association. It's a ripple effect: by working together, you borrow each other's credibility and introduce your brands to new, aligned audiences. **Partnerships and collaborations can exponentially grow your audience's trust** because people are more likely to trust you if someone they already respect is vouching for you.

But collaborations aren't just about expanding your reach—they also show your audience that you're part of a broader network, that you value relationships, and that you're committed to bringing the best possible resources to them. Working with others signals that you're secure in your expertise, willing to share the spotlight, and constantly seeking new ways to add value.

Choosing the Right Partners

Not all partnerships are created equal. Collaborating with the right people or brands is crucial to ensuring that the relationship is beneficial for both parties and resonates with your audience. Here are some strategies for choosing the right collaborators:

1. **Align Values and Audience**
   The most successful collaborations happen when both parties have similar values and complementary audiences. Look for partners whose mission and goals align with your own. For example, if you're a wellness coach, collaborating with a brand that sells health-conscious products could be a great fit. Your audiences should overlap in meaningful ways—this ensures that your collaboration feels natural and that the content resonates with both of your followers.

- *Tip*: Before reaching out, research potential partners to make sure their brand aligns with yours. Ask yourself: *Do we have a shared purpose? Would our audiences benefit from this partnership?*

2. **Focus on Authentic Relationships**

    Authenticity is key when it comes to collaborations. The best partnerships are those built on genuine relationships, not just transactional interactions. Start by building relationships with peers in your industry by engaging with their content, offering support, and showing genuine interest in their work. When the time comes to collaborate, the relationship feels organic rather than forced.

    - *Example*: Rather than cold emailing a potential partner with a request to collaborate, spend time interacting with their content first. Comment on their posts, share their work, and get to know them. This builds a foundation of trust, so when you do reach out for a partnership, they're more likely to be receptive.

3. **Look for Complementary Strengths**

    Collaborations work best when each partner brings something unique to the table. Instead of partnering with someone who does exactly what you do, look for complementary strengths. For example, if you're great at creating content but need help with marketing, partnering with someone who excels at promotion could be a win-win. This allows both parties to contribute their best skills while benefiting from each other's expertise.

- o *Tip*: When approaching a potential partner, highlight what you bring to the table and how the collaboration can benefit both of you. Show that you've thought about their needs as well as your own.

Real-World Examples: Women Who Built Their Reputations Through Collaboration

Collaboration has been a game-changer for many successful women, allowing them to grow their brands, reach new audiences, and build deeper trust with their followers.

Example 1: Sophia Amoruso and Nasty Gal
Sophia Amoruso, the founder of Nasty Gal and later Girlboss, built her empire largely through strategic collaborations with influencers and like-minded entrepreneurs. Early on, she partnered with fashion bloggers and influencers whose audiences aligned with her edgy, vintage-inspired fashion brand. These partnerships not only helped her reach new customers but also positioned Nasty Gal as a brand that was part of a larger, trendsetting community. By collaborating with trusted voices in the fashion space, Sophia built credibility and expanded her brand's influence quickly.

Example 2: Marie Forleo and Danielle LaPorte
Marie Forleo, a business coach and author, has built a strong network of collaborators over the years. One of her most successful partnerships was with Danielle LaPorte, another influential author and entrepreneur. The two women joined forces to offer joint webinars and cross-promoted each other's

programs to their audiences. Because their values aligned, and both had built trust with their respective communities, their collaboration was a natural fit and allowed both women to grow their reach while offering even more value to their followers.

These examples show that successful collaborations are built on mutual respect, shared values, and a genuine commitment to helping each other succeed. When done well, partnerships can enhance your brand, build your credibility, and deepen trust with your audience.

How to Approach Potential Collaborators

Approaching potential collaborators can feel intimidating, but with the right mindset and preparation, you can create mutually beneficial relationships that elevate both of your brands. Here's how to approach potential partners:

1. **Start with Value**
   When reaching out to potential collaborators, focus on the value you can offer them. Rather than making the request solely about what you stand to gain, highlight how the collaboration can benefit both parties. Be clear about what you bring to the table and how the partnership will serve their audience as well as your own.

   o *Example*: Instead of saying, "I'd love to collaborate with you because you have a large following," try, "I think our audiences would really benefit from hearing your expertise on [topic], and I'd love to create something together that provides value to both our communities."

2. **Be Specific About the Collaboration**
Before reaching out, have a clear idea of what the collaboration could look like. Whether it's a joint webinar, a guest blog post, or co-hosting a social media event, the more specific you are, the easier it will be for the other person to envision how the partnership will work. This shows that you've thought through the details and are serious about making the collaboration successful.

    o *Tip*: Propose a specific idea for the collaboration, but leave room for flexibility. For example, "I was thinking we could co-host a webinar on [topic], but I'm open to other ideas if there's something you think would be a better fit."

3. **Focus on Long-Term Relationships**
While one-off collaborations can be beneficial, it's even more powerful to build long-term partnerships. When you focus on building an ongoing relationship, the collaboration feels more authentic, and your audiences will start to see you as part of a trusted network. Look for opportunities to collaborate with the same people over time, whether through multiple projects or by continuing to support each other's work.

    o *Tip*: After a successful collaboration, follow up to express your gratitude and explore future opportunities. This helps keep the relationship strong and opens the door for more collaborations down the road.

4. **Be Professional and Respectful**
   When reaching out to potential collaborators, be professional and respectful of their time. If they don't respond right away, don't take it personally. People are often busy, and it may take some time for them to consider your proposal. Always be gracious, whether they accept the collaboration or not, and keep the door open for future opportunities.

   o *Tip*: Send a polite follow-up if you haven't heard back in a week or two. Keep it short and respectful, such as, "I just wanted to follow up on my last message to see if you had any thoughts on collaborating. No rush—looking forward to hearing from you when you have a moment!"

Practical Tips for Building Mutually Beneficial Relationships

1. **Engage with Potential Partners Before Reaching Out**
   Before you propose a collaboration, engage with your potential partner's content. Comment on their posts, share their work, and show genuine interest in what they're doing. This builds rapport and makes your eventual proposal feel more natural.

2. **Keep Communication Clear and Open**
   Transparency is key to any successful partnership. Be

clear about your expectations, timelines, and what you hope to achieve. This ensures that both parties are on the same page and reduces the risk of misunderstandings.

3. **Follow Up After the Collaboration**
After the collaboration, follow up to thank your partner and share the results of your joint efforts. Celebrate the success of the partnership, and offer to continue supporting their work in the future. This helps solidify the relationship and opens the door for future opportunities.

Key Takeaway: Collaborations Build Trust and Expand Influence

Collaborating with trusted peers and brands is one of the most powerful ways to grow your audience, build credibility, and deepen trust. By forming authentic partnerships, you can leverage shared audiences, offer more value to your followers, and create meaningful connections that benefit everyone involved. In the world of online growth, trust through partnerships is a powerful strategy that amplifies your impact.

In the next chapter, we'll explore how to measure your success, both in terms of audience engagement and the trust you've built, to ensure that your efforts are leading to sustainable growth.

CHAPTER 9:
Measuring Your Impact and Growing with Integrity

As you build your online presence and grow your audience, it's natural to want to measure your success. Numbers—likes, shares, followers—can give you an indication of how well you're doing, but true growth is about much more than just metrics. **Data can guide your growth, but integrity should guide your actions.** The real measure of success is how deeply you connect with your audience and how much they trust you. **Building trust with your audience isn't just about numbers; it's about meaningful interactions** that resonate long after someone has clicked the "like" button.

The Balance Between Data and Meaningful Engagement

In the digital world, it's easy to become fixated on vanity metrics—likes, follower counts, shares, and views. While these numbers can offer some insight into your reach, they don't tell the full story. The real value lies in **engagement**—how your audience is interacting with your content, how they feel about your brand, and whether they're taking meaningful actions like commenting, sharing their stories, or becoming loyal customers.

The goal is to build a community where your audience feels heard, valued, and connected. This is where **integrity** comes in. Growth for the sake of numbers alone can lead you down a path of inauthenticity—chasing trends, buying followers, or pushing content that doesn't align with your values. However, **growing with integrity** means staying true to your mission, even if it takes longer. It's about focusing on long-term trust rather than short-term numbers.

How to Measure Engagement Beyond Likes and Shares

To grow your audience with integrity, you need to focus on metrics that measure the depth of engagement rather than just the breadth of your reach. Here are a few ways to measure your impact more meaningfully:

1. **Comments and Conversations**
   One of the strongest indicators of engagement is the number of meaningful conversations happening in response to your content. Comments, direct messages, and community discussions show that your audience is actively engaging with your ideas. Pay attention to the quality of these interactions—are people sharing their thoughts, asking questions, or seeking advice? Are they investing time in a dialogue with you or with other members of your community?

- *Tip*: Track how often your content sparks conversations. Look for posts where people are not just liking but also sharing their own experiences, asking follow-up questions, or tagging others. These deeper interactions are a sign that your message is resonating.

2. **Shares and Recommendations**
When someone shares your content or recommends you to their followers, they're putting their own credibility on the line to support you. This is a major indicator of trust and engagement. If people are regularly sharing your posts or telling others about your brand, it shows that they find real value in what you offer.

    - *Example*: Instead of focusing only on the number of likes a post gets, track how often your content is shared. This is a better measure of how much your audience trusts your message enough to pass it along.

3. **Time Spent on Content**
Metrics like video views or blog post reads can tell you how many people have seen your content, but what's more important is how much time they're spending with it. Are they watching your videos to the end? Are they reading your articles thoroughly? High engagement time means your content is holding their attention, and they find it valuable enough to stick around.

- *Tip*: Use tools like Google Analytics to measure time spent on your website or YouTube analytics to track watch times. This will give you insight into how engaging your content is beyond just the initial click.

4. **Repeat Engagement**
Returning visitors, repeat customers, and regular commenters are all indicators of a loyal audience. These are the people who consistently find value in your work and keep coming back for more. The goal isn't just to attract people once, but to build a relationship that brings them back again and again.

   - *Tip*: Track how often the same people engage with your content over time. Are there names you see frequently in your comment section or emails? These repeat interactions are a strong indicator of loyalty and trust.

Stories of Growth by Focusing on Meaning Over Metrics

Many successful women have grown their online presence not by focusing on vanity metrics but by prioritizing **meaningful engagement** and integrity in their actions.

Example 1: Brené Brown's Focus on Connection
Brené Brown, a researcher and speaker on vulnerability and courage, didn't start with millions of followers. Instead, she built her audience by creating deeply personal and valuable content that resonated with people on a meaningful level. Brené didn't chase trends or worry about follower counts; she focused on creating genuine connections with her audience.

By staying true to her message and sharing her own struggles and stories, she built an incredibly loyal community of people who trusted her. Today, Brené has a massive following, but her success is rooted in her ability to create meaningful interactions, not in chasing numbers.

Example 2: Jenna Kutcher's Pivot to Purposeful Growth
Entrepreneur Jenna Kutcher initially grew her online presence by sharing beautiful photos and polished content. However, she realized that this strategy wasn't leading to the kind of deep engagement she wanted. Jenna decided to shift her focus from building a large follower count to creating a more personal connection with her audience. She began sharing more vulnerable stories about her struggles with body image, motherhood, and entrepreneurship. As a result, her audience became more engaged, sharing their own stories and building a community around her brand. Jenna's growth became about **depth**, not just **reach**, which ultimately strengthened her trustworthiness.

Growing with Integrity: Ethical Strategies for Sustainable Growth

As you measure your success and refine your strategies, it's crucial to ensure that your growth remains ethical and aligned with your values. Here are some tips for growing with integrity:

1. **Avoid Vanity Metrics**
   It's tempting to focus on the numbers that are easiest to track—likes, views, follower counts—but these metrics don't necessarily reflect true engagement. Prioritize metrics that measure trust

and loyalty, like comments, shares, and time spent on your content. Remember, a smaller, highly engaged audience is far more valuable than a large, disengaged one.

- o *Tip*: Resist the urge to inflate your numbers by buying followers or using gimmicky tactics. Authentic growth takes time, but it's the only way to build real, lasting trust.

2. **Stay Aligned with Your Values**
As you grow, it can be tempting to follow trends or adopt strategies that promise quick success. However, it's important to stay true to your core values. Whether you're creating content, launching new products, or partnering with others, always ask yourself, *Does this align with my mission?* If the answer is no, it's not worth the short-term gain.

- o *Tip*: Revisit your mission statement regularly to ensure that your growth strategies are aligned with your purpose. Growth that compromises your integrity will erode trust in the long run.

3. **Provide Genuine Value**
Growth should never come at the expense of your audience's trust. Ensure that every piece of content you create provides genuine value. This means prioritizing quality over quantity and staying focused on how you can serve your audience's needs, rather than just growing your numbers.

- *Example*: Instead of trying to post every day just to stay visible, focus on creating fewer but more impactful posts that resonate deeply with your audience. Your community will value the quality of your content more than its frequency.

4. **Engage Authentically**

    Your interactions with your audience should always be authentic. Don't just engage to boost your metrics—engage because you genuinely care about your community. Respond to comments, ask meaningful questions, and build real relationships with your followers.

    - *Tip*: Dedicate time each week to engage with your audience in a personal way—whether it's replying to comments, answering direct messages, or asking for feedback. Authentic engagement builds lasting relationships and trust.

Practical Tools for Measuring Trust and Engagement

1. **Google Analytics**

    Google Analytics is a powerful tool for tracking how people are engaging with your website. It can help you measure metrics like time spent on pages, bounce rate, and return visitors—giving you insight into how well your content is resonating with your audience.

2. **Instagram Insights/Facebook Analytics**

    Social media platforms offer built-in analytics tools

that can give you deeper insights into your audience's behavior. Track metrics like post reach, engagement rate, and shares to see which types of content are building the most connection with your audience.

3. **Survey Tools (Typeform, Google Forms)**
   If you want to measure how much your audience trusts you or what they find valuable about your content, consider sending out surveys. Tools like Typeform and Google Forms allow you to collect feedback directly from your audience, giving you qualitative data to complement your quantitative metrics.

4. **Email Marketing Platforms (Mailchimp, ConvertKit)**
   If you have an email list, platforms like Mailchimp and ConvertKit allow you to track open rates, click-through rates, and engagement with your emails. This can help you measure how well your messaging resonates with your audience and whether they're taking action based on your content.

Key Takeaway: Integrity Leads to Lasting Growth

At the heart of lasting success is trust, and trust can't be measured solely by numbers. By focusing on meaningful engagement, staying aligned with your values, and growing with integrity, you'll build a community that believes in you, supports you, and grows with you. Remember, it's not just about how many people are following you—it's about how deeply you're connecting with them.

In the next chapter, we'll discuss how to keep this momentum going, ensuring that your community remains engaged and loyal as you grow your brand sustainably over time.

CHAPTER 10:
Maintaining Momentum and Building Trust for the Long Term

Building trust online is not a one-time achievement—it's an ongoing relationship that requires consistent care and attention. While the strategies you've implemented so far have helped you grow a loyal audience, the real challenge is **maintaining** that trust over the long term. **Trust is an ongoing relationship**, and keeping your audience engaged requires dedication to both consistency and authenticity. **To keep winning hearts and minds, consistency and authenticity must remain central to your online presence**, even as your brand evolves and grows.

Trust as a Long-Term Relationship

Think of trust as a garden. It flourishes with regular care—watering, pruning, and nurturing—but can quickly wither if neglected. The same principle applies to the trust you've built with your audience. It's not enough to simply gain their attention; you must continue to provide value, connect authentically, and show up consistently over time.

The challenge many creators and entrepreneurs face is **how to maintain that momentum** without burning out or losing sight of what originally made their audience trust them. Growth is exciting, but with growth comes the pressure to keep up, stay relevant, and continue delivering at a high level. The key to long-term success is finding balance: how can you keep nurturing your audience while ensuring that you, too, stay energized and inspired?

Staying Relevant Without Burnout

One of the greatest risks for creators as they grow is **burnout**. The pressure to consistently produce new, high-quality content while managing the demands of running a brand or business can be overwhelming. Burnout not only affects your mental and emotional well-being, but it can also impact the quality of your content and the connection you have with your audience. If you're not careful, the passion that once fueled your work can start to feel like a burden.

To avoid burnout while staying relevant, you need to strike a balance between providing value to your audience and taking care of yourself. **Sustainability** should be at the heart of your long-term strategy. This means creating a system that allows you to keep showing up consistently without exhausting your energy or creativity.

Stories of Long-Term Influencers Who Kept Their Communities Engaged

Many successful influencers have managed to maintain a loyal following over the years by staying true to their mission while evolving with their audience.

Example 1: Marie Forleo

Marie Forleo, the founder of MarieTV and B-School, has been a trusted voice in the entrepreneurial space for over a decade. Her success stems from her unwavering commitment to delivering consistent, high-quality content while evolving with the needs of her audience. Whether through her YouTube channel, podcast, or courses, Marie has continued to show up authentically, sharing both her expertise and her personal journey. By staying consistent and adapting to her audience's evolving challenges, she has managed to grow her community while maintaining a deep level of trust.

Example 2: Pat Flynn

Pat Flynn, founder of Smart Passive Income, has built a loyal audience by providing valuable, transparent advice on building online businesses. Pat's success comes from his commitment to his audience—he consistently shows up with content that provides real value and never shies away from sharing his failures as well as his successes. By being open about his journey and staying consistent in his delivery, Pat has earned the long-term trust of his followers, many of whom have been with him since the beginning.

Both Marie and Pat understood that to keep their audiences engaged for the long term, they needed to remain authentic, consistent, and responsive to their community's needs. Their ability to grow while maintaining the core of their message is what has allowed them to build lasting trust with their audiences.

Practical Tips for Developing a Long-Term Strategy

1. **Create a Sustainable Content Calendar**
    A long-term strategy requires planning ahead and pacing

yourself. A **content calendar** helps you map out your content in a way that keeps you consistent without overwhelming yourself. Start by planning your content on a monthly or quarterly basis, balancing educational or value-driven content with more personal or behind-the-scenes posts. This ensures you have a steady flow of content without feeling like you're constantly scrambling for new ideas.

- *Tip*: Use a tool like Trello, Asana, or Google Calendar to plan your content. Block off time each week to create or schedule posts in advance, so you're never left rushing at the last minute.

2. **Build in Breaks and Time for Reflection**
   Burnout is a real threat, and part of maintaining momentum is knowing when to step back. Schedule breaks into your calendar where you can rest, reflect, and recharge. These breaks will allow you to come back stronger and more creative, ensuring that your content remains fresh and authentic.

   - *Tip*: Take regular digital detoxes or time off from social media. Let your audience know in advance when you'll be stepping away, and come back with renewed energy and ideas. Your audience will appreciate your transparency and the quality of content you bring when you return.

3. **Evolve with Your Audience**
   Your audience's needs will change over time, and it's important to evolve alongside them. Stay engaged by

regularly asking your community for feedback, whether through polls, Q&As, or email surveys. This will help you understand what they're struggling with and how you can continue to provide value. Be willing to pivot your content or offerings based on what your audience is asking for.

- o *Tip*: Set aside time each quarter to review your audience engagement and reflect on what's working and what isn't. Are there certain types of content that get more interaction? Are your followers asking for more of something specific? Use this feedback to inform your strategy moving forward.

4. **Stay True to Your Core Message**
While it's important to adapt to changing trends and audience needs, never lose sight of your core message and values. Authenticity is what drew your audience to you in the first place, and it's what will keep them with you. As your brand grows, stay grounded in the mission and values that originally built your community's trust.

- o *Tip*: Revisit your mission statement regularly. If you're ever unsure of whether to pursue a new opportunity or direction, ask yourself: *Does this align with my core values?* Staying true to your message will help ensure that your growth remains authentic and sustainable.

5. **Foster Deeper Engagement**
One of the best ways to maintain momentum is by creating opportunities for deeper engagement within

your community. Move beyond surface-level interactions and build genuine connections by fostering conversation, collaboration, and community involvement. This could mean hosting live events, starting a private community group, or inviting your followers to share their stories or experiences.

- o *Tip*: Consider starting a Facebook group or Slack channel where your most loyal followers can connect with you and each other. This helps deepen relationships and makes your audience feel like they're part of something bigger than just a social media account.

Key Takeaway: Trust is Built Through Consistency and Authenticity

As you continue to grow your online presence, remember that trust is built over time and through consistent, meaningful interactions. **Maintaining momentum** means showing up regularly, delivering value, and staying authentic to who you are. Growth with integrity is not a sprint, but a marathon—sustainable, thoughtful, and rooted in genuine connection.

By developing a long-term strategy that balances content creation with personal well-being, evolving with your audience, and staying true to your core message, you can keep winning the hearts and minds of your community for years to come.

In the final section, we'll reflect on the journey of building an online presence rooted in trust and offer some final thoughts on how to keep growing with authenticity and purpose.

CONCLUSION:
Building a Legacy of Trust

In many ways, the story of Emily James embodies everything we've explored throughout this book. Emily, a freelance graphic designer, started her online journey much like many of us do—unsure of where to begin and overwhelmed by the fast pace of social media. She followed the trends, focused on building a large following, and struggled to stand out in an increasingly crowded space. For a while, she chased numbers, tweaking her content to attract more likes and shares, but something wasn't clicking. Despite her growing follower count, she felt disconnected from her audience. The numbers didn't translate into meaningful interactions or genuine connections.

It wasn't until Emily shifted her focus from growing a following to building **trust** that things began to change. She started sharing more personal stories, revealing the challenges she faced in building her business, and connecting with her audience on a deeper, more authentic level. She moved beyond the surface-level engagement of likes and comments and started asking her followers about their own journeys, their struggles, and their dreams. By embracing vulnerability, showing up consistently, and staying true to her values, Emily transformed her online presence. She no longer chased numbers—instead, she cultivated a loyal, engaged community that trusted her, valued her, and championed her work. Today, Emily's business thrives, and her audience supports her in ways she never imagined.

The Foundations of Winning Hearts and Minds Online

Throughout this book, we've explored how to build trust, grow your audience, and create lasting relationships online. **Trust, authenticity, and consistency** are the foundations of winning hearts and minds online. As Emily's story illustrates, when you shift your focus away from vanity metrics and instead invest in meaningful interactions, you unlock the true potential of your online presence.

Here's a recap of the key lessons we've covered in this journey:

- **Laying the Foundation**: Trust is the cornerstone of every successful online relationship. Building trust requires authenticity, consistency, and a commitment to showing up for your audience, not just once but over time.

- **Crafting an Authentic Digital Persona**: Your authenticity is what sets you apart. By aligning your values with your online presence and sharing your personal journey, you build connections that resonate deeply with your audience.

- **Defining Your Audience and Niche**: Knowing who you're speaking to allows you to refine your message and build a stronger connection with your community. By identifying your audience's needs and pain points, you can create content that speaks directly to their challenges.

- **The Art of Storytelling**: Stories are powerful tools for building trust and deepening relationships. By sharing your personal experiences and framing them in a way that reflects your audience's journey, you create emotional connections that last.

- **Engaging Through Consistent Communication**: Consistency builds reliability, and reliability builds trust. By maintaining a regular, transparent line of communication with your audience, you create a sense of community that fosters loyalty.

- **Building Communities, Not Just Followers**: A loyal community is more powerful than a large but disengaged following. By focusing on creating private, intimate spaces where trust deepens, you can cultivate a thriving community that supports and advocates for you.

- **Handling Criticism and Negative Feedback Gracefully**: Trust is tested in how you respond to criticism. By addressing negative feedback with grace and humility, you can build credibility and deepen the trust of your audience.

- **Collaborations and Networking**: Partnering with trusted peers can exponentially grow your audience's trust. Authentic collaborations allow you to leverage shared audiences while maintaining the integrity of your message.

- **Measuring Your Impact and Growing with Integrity**: Data can guide your growth, but integrity should guide your actions. Focusing on meaningful engagement, rather than vanity metrics, ensures that your growth is sustainable and rooted in trust.

- **Maintaining Momentum**: Trust is not a one-time achievement; it's an ongoing relationship. Consistency, authenticity, and staying true to your core values will keep your audience engaged and loyal for the long term.

A Call to Action: Your 90-Day Plan to Build Trust

As you've seen throughout this book, building trust and creating a loyal online community doesn't happen overnight, but it's a journey well worth taking. Now, it's time to put these lessons into action and build an online presence rooted in trust, authenticity, and consistency. Over the next 90 days, commit to implementing the strategies you've learned:

- **Define Your Audience**: Spend time getting to know your audience, their pain points, and what they need most from you. Create content that speaks directly to those needs.

- **Show Up Authentically**: Share your personal stories, show your audience who you are behind the scenes, and align your content with your core values. Authenticity will always resonate more than perfection.

- **Engage Consistently**: Create a content calendar that allows you to show up regularly without burning out. Stay consistent, but don't be afraid to take breaks when needed—your audience will appreciate your honesty.

- **Focus on Building Community**: Move beyond the pursuit of followers and focus on building a loyal community. Whether through a private group, an email list, or regular live interactions, create spaces where trust can flourish.

- **Handle Feedback with Grace**: When criticism comes, and it will, handle it with humility and openness. See every piece of feedback as an opportunity to grow and connect more deeply with your audience.

By committing to these steps over the next 90 days, you'll begin to see the transformation in how your audience engages with you. More importantly, you'll be building a foundation of trust that will support your brand for years to come.

Your journey starts now. Whether you're just beginning to grow your online presence or you've been building your brand for years, the path forward is clear: trust, authenticity, and consistency. These are the values that will win you not just followers, but loyal supporters who believe in your mission, trust your voice, and are ready to champion your success.

Now, go out there and start building your legacy of trust!

!

BOOKS IN THIS SERIES:
The Course Creator's Toolkit

The Course Creator's Toolkit series is designed for course creators who want to craft engaging, high-value courses that stand out in the crowded online education market. Based on real-world challenges faced by my clients, these books offer practical, step-by-step solutions to common pitfalls like low engagement, weak course design, or unclear outcomes.

Each chapter in the series feels like a personal coaching session with me, Meek Dual. I am passionate about helping others package their expertise into courses that not only sell but transform lives. You'll learn how to create interactive learning experiences, market your courses effectively, and build communities that keep learners engaged.

If you're ready to avoid the mistakes that hold most course creators back and build a profitable, high-perceived value course, this series is your blueprint for success.

Book 1: The Authority Advantage: Build Your Influence, Impact, and Income by Sharing What You Know

Are you ready to transform your expertise into influence, impact, and income?

In The Authority Advantage, entrepreneur and success coach Meek Dual reveals the proven strategies to help you become the go-to expert in your field. Whether you're an entrepreneur, coach, consultant, or creative professional, this book is your step-by-step guide to building lasting authority by leveraging the skills and knowledge you already possess.

Drawing from her own experiences and the journeys of countless successful clients, Meek shows you exactly how to:

- Find Your Zone of Genius: Identify the unique strengths that set you apart from the competition.

- Build a Personal Brand: Craft a brand that resonates with your ideal audience and communicates your value.

- Package Your Expertise: Turn your knowledge into profitable products and services, from online courses to consulting packages.

- Expand Your Influence: Use content creation and public speaking to grow your authority and reach more people.

- Stay Relevant: Learn how to continuously evolve as an expert and adapt to industry trends.

This book is packed with practical exercises, real-life case studies, and actionable steps that will help you create a legacy of influence while generating new income streams. You don't have to be a celebrity or a seasoned speaker to build authority. With the right mindset, tools, and persistence, anyone can become the expert others turn to for guidance and solutions.

Ready to amplify your authority and take your business to the next level?

Whether you're just starting out or you're ready to scale your impact, The Authority Advantage will give you the roadmap to success.

Get your copy today and start building the influence, impact, and income you deserve!

Book 2: Course Creator's Gold: Build Interactive Courses that Stick and SELL

Are you ready to transform your expertise into an engaging, high-value online course that captivates learners and generates revenue?

Course Creator's Gold is your step-by-step guide to creating courses that not only teach but inspire real transformation.

Packed with practical strategies and insights from my years of experience helping clients overcome the common pitfalls of course creation, this book is like having a personal coaching session with me, Meek Dual. I've helped countless women course creators who struggled with flat, disengaging content, unclear goals, and low sales. Now, I'm sharing the proven techniques that can help you avoid these challenges and build a course that not only sells but creates lasting impact.

Inside Course Creator's Gold, you'll learn:

- How to design interactive and dynamic learning experiences that keep your students engaged.

- Proven methods for crafting clear, actionable course goals that motivate learners.

- Practical tips for marketing your course and positioning it as a must-have solution in a crowded market.

- Strategies for building a supportive community around your course that fosters long-term engagement.

Whether you're just getting started or looking to refine your current course, Course Creator's Gold gives you the tools to create an online course that sells and delights learners. Start your journey toward course creation success today!

Book 3: Followers to Friends: Build Authentic Connections and Lasting Success Online

Ready to turn your followers into loyal, engaged supporters who trust and champion your brand?

In *Followers to Friends*, success coach and creative visionary Meek Dual reveals the step-by-step strategies you need to build real, lasting connections online. Whether you're an entrepreneur, content creator, or professional seeking to grow your influence, this book is your roadmap to transforming followers into a true community—one rooted in trust and authenticity.

It's not about vanity metrics—it's about building trust. Through practical insights, real-life stories, and actionable steps, Meek shows you exactly how to:

- Build Trust: Learn why trust is the foundation of all online success and how to earn it through authenticity and consistency.

- Share Your Story: Craft an authentic digital persona that resonates deeply with your audience.

- Create Lasting Engagement: Develop strategies that encourage meaningful interactions and keep your audience coming back for more.

- Grow a Loyal Community: Move beyond just gaining followers and focus on building a supportive, engaged group of true fans.

- Handle Criticism with Grace: Turn negative feedback into opportunities for deeper connection and credibility.

With Meek's expert guidance, you'll learn how to build a sustainable online presence that doesn't just attract followers—it turns them into friends, loyal customers, and advocates for your brand. Packed with practical exercises and actionable advice, this book provides the tools you need to create real, lasting impact in the digital world.

Plus, as a bonus, you can access the FREE companion workbook to help you put these strategies into action and track your progress over the next 90 days.

Are you ready to transform your online presence and build a community that lasts?

Get your copy of *Followers to Friends* today and start building the authentic connections that lead to lasting success!

ABOUT THE AUTHOR

Meek Dual is a success coach, storyteller, and creative visionary dedicated to helping individuals and businesses build authentic connections that drive lasting success. Known for her unique blend of storytelling, content creation, and strategic thinking, Meek has helped entrepreneurs, influencers, and creators around the world turn followers into loyal, engaged communities.

As the founder of a thriving personal brand and creative business, Meek has mastered the art of building trust online, not just through polished content, but through genuine relationships that resonate deeply with her audience. Her clients and followers often speak of "Meek's Magic"—her ability to create content that not only inspires but also leads to meaningful engagement and real results.

But Meek's journey wasn't easy. As a single mother raising children with learning challenges, she learned how to navigate obstacles with resilience, faith, and determination. Through her own experiences, she developed a deep understanding of how to balance personal struggles with the pursuit of professional excellence. It's this journey that has shaped her into the empathetic, driven coach and leader she is today.

In addition to coaching, Meek is a sought-after speaker, educator, and content creator who regularly shares her insights on building personal brands, creating digital products, and fostering loyal online communities. She believes in the power of authentic connections and is passionate about helping others unlock their potential to grow their influence while staying true to their values.

When she's not working with clients or creating content, Meek enjoys spending time with her family, continuing her personal development journey, and inspiring others to achieve their dreams—one authentic connection at a time.

For more tools, resources, and free content to help you grow your own online community, visit meekdual.com.

www.ingramcontent.com/pod-product-compliance
Lightning Source LLC
Chambersburg PA
CBHW071101240526
45471CB00016B/2295